Doing Your Part

Serving Your Community

Kelly Rodgers

Consultant

Caryn Williams, M.S.Ed.
Madison County Schools
Huntsville, AL

Image Credits: Cover & p.1 Leland Bobbé/Corbis/age fotostock; p.10 (left) Ariel Skelley/Blend Images/Alamy; pp.24–25, 26–27 Blend Images/Alamy; p.7 (top right) Blue Jean Images/Alamy; p.25 (right) Hill Street Studios/Blend Images/Alamy; pp.4–5, 23 Marmaduke St. John/Alamy; pp.15 (middle), 32 Richard Green/Alamy; p.13 (top) VStock/Alamy; pp.6, 10 (right) Jim West/age fotostock; p.12 Alex J. Berliner/Associated Press; p.21 (right) Peter Beck/Corbis; p.11 Brian Babineau/NBAE/Getty Images; p.15 (bottom) John Moore/Getty Images; p.29 (top) Michael H/Digital Vision/Getty Images; pp.2, 7 (top left & both bottom), p.4 (bottom), pp.9 (top & middle), p.28 (top) iStock; p.19 Lexa Hoang; pp.16-17 Amanda McCoy/MCT/Newscom; p.29 (bottom) Jim West/Image Broker/Newscom; p.17 (top) Mark & Audrey Gibson/Stock Connection Worldwide/Newscom; p.21 (left) Nils Hendrik Muller/Cultura/Newscom; pp.14–15 Paul J. Richards/AFP/Getty Images/Newscom; p.31 Zero Creatives/Cultural/Newscom; all other images from Shutterstock.

Teacher Created Materials
5301 Oceanus Drive
Huntington Beach, CA 92649-1030
http://www.tcmpub.com

ISBN 978-1-4333-7367-1

Printed by: 590835
Printed in: China

Table of Contents

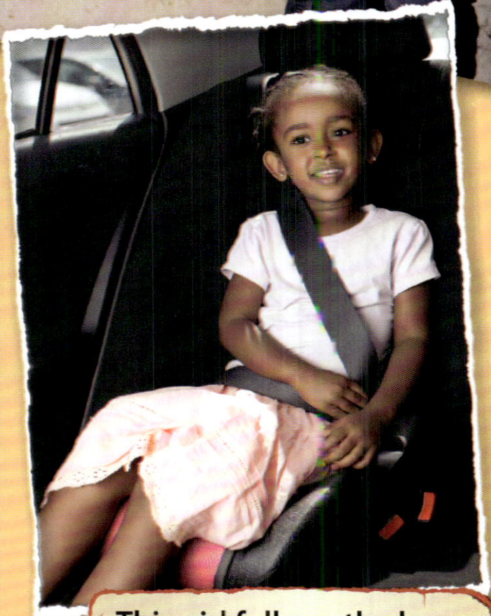

This girl follows the law by buckling her seat belt.

Responsible Citizens

American **citizens** are members of our country. We all have **rights**. These are things that all people should be able to do and to have. We are free. We can think what we want and we can say what we believe. The U.S. Constitution (kon-sti-TOO-shuhn) protects these rights.

These kids are being responsible citizens by listening to the crossing guard.

Our Constitution

The U.S. Constitution is the main set of laws for America. It says how our government works. And it lists our rights. It says "we the people" are in charge of America.

Along with rights, we have **responsibilities** (ri-spon-suh-BIL-i-teez). These are our duties, or things we should do. Good citizens are responsible. They support the U.S. Constitution. They follow the rules. They do not break the laws. They respect the rights and beliefs of others. They take part in our government. Responsible citizens work to make their country better.

Community

We live in communities (kuh-MYOO-ni-teez). We go to school and we play sports on teams. We shop in stores and eat in restaurants. We visit libraries and walk through parks. All these places make up a community.

People in communities are not always the same. We may not all wear the same clothes. We may not eat all the same foods. But we all share certain goals. We all want to make our communities better places to live.

Some communities are small. Others are large. But many communities make up our nation. When we help our communities, we are being good citizens.

These people help build homes for people in New Orleans.

store

family

These are parts of a community.

sports team

park

Learning How to Do Your Part

There are many ways to learn how to do your part. Our communities have rules to help us learn what to do. There are rules for our homes and rules for our schools. Our country has rules, too. These are called *laws*. Some laws are found in the U.S. Constitution. Others can be found on signs or in books. Laws help us know how to be good members of our community. Following the law is an important part of being a good citizen.

You can also learn from people in your community. You can listen to your parents and talk to your teachers. They will show you ways to be a good citizen and how to help in your community. This book will also help you learn!

Signs in our communities remind us to follow the laws.

This family follows the law by wearing helmets.

This girl follows the rules at school by raising her hand.

Ways to Help

Helping the community is part of being a good citizen. You can help people and keep your community clean. You can treat others fairly. These are all great ways to help!

Volunteer

People have to work hard to make their communities great. Community leaders do some of this work, but **volunteers** play a big part, too. This means that they do the work for free. They do it because they want to be good citizens.

Volunteers do not get money for their work, but they do get something in return. They make new friends and learn how to do new things. They learn to be a part of a team. And they help build better communities. It feels good to help others. By volunteering, you can help make the world a better place.

These people volunteer to build a house.

Some people volunteer at soup kitchens, where people can eat for free.

Food Banks

A food bank is like a store but its food is free. It is for people in need who do not have money to buy food. Food banks need volunteers. They need people to help sort and box food.

Donate

Every community has people who need help. They may have lost their jobs. They may not be able to feed their families. They may not have a place to live. Sometimes people get very sick. They may not be able to take care of themselves. These people need help.

Rico Rodriguez raises money for Share Our Strength.

Share Our Strength

Share Our Strength is a charity that helps hungry children. There are almost 13 million hungry children in America. Share Our Strength helps get food to children in need.

There are many ways to reach out to those in need. There are local **charities** (CHAR-i-teez). These are groups that help people in need. People can **donate**, or give, to these charities. Some people donate money. The charities can use it to buy food, medicine, and clothing.

Some people donate items, such as clothing or food. Some charities take furniture (FUR-ni-cher), toys, and books. They give these things to people who need them. Donating helps make a community stronger. And it feels good to know that you are helping people in need.

This girl donates canned food for a food drive.

People can donate food and supplies to charities.

Each year, **natural disasters** hit America. These are things such as floods and fires. These disasters can happen quickly. Sometimes there is no warning. They leave lots of people in need. It is important for everyone to help when a disaster strikes.

Sometimes people do not know how to help. They might want to donate food or clothing. But they may not know how to get things to people across the country. **Relief** groups work to get supplies to people who need them. The Red Cross is a relief group. It takes donations. Then, it gives them to people in need. The Red Cross even helps people in other countries.

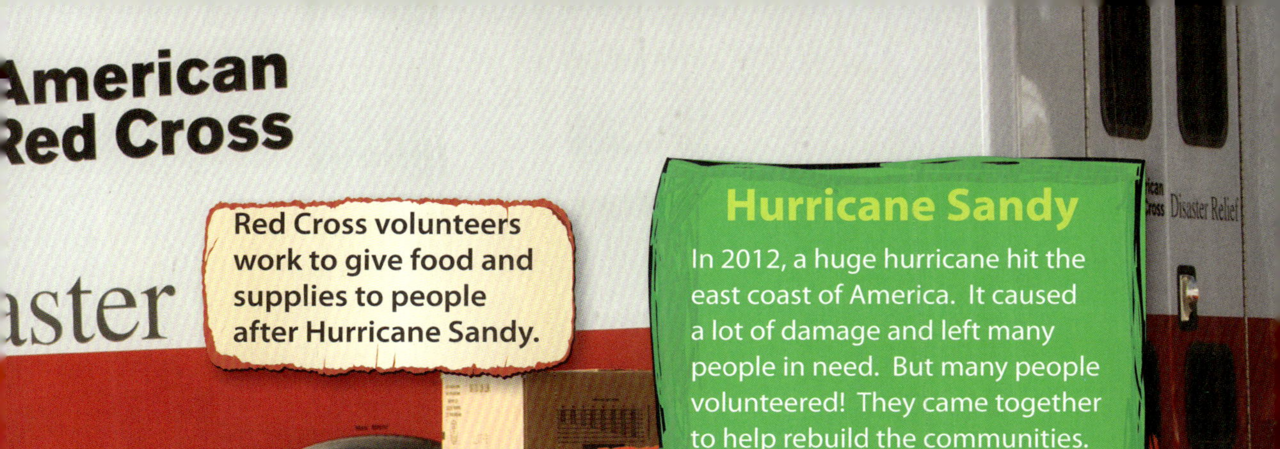

Red Cross volunteers work to give food and supplies to people after Hurricane Sandy.

Hurricane Sandy

In 2012, a huge hurricane hit the east coast of America. It caused a lot of damage and left many people in need. But many people volunteered! They came together to help rebuild the communities.

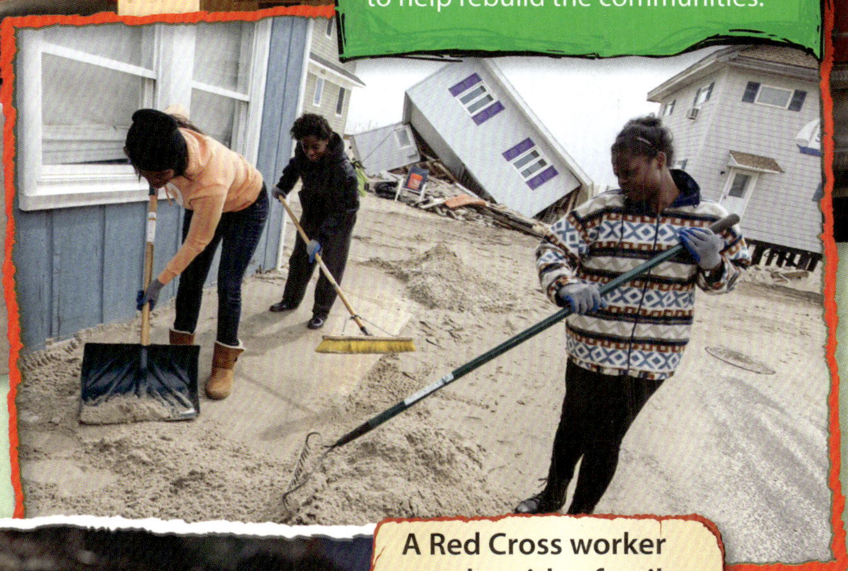

A Red Cross worker speaks with a family after a flood in 2012.

Keep It Clean

Public places are areas that everyone can use. Have you ever built a sand castle on a beach or gone swimming in the ocean? Maybe you have hiked through a forest or had a fun family picnic in a park? These are all public places. Public places are a big part of communities. They are there for everyone to enjoy. It is important to keep these public places clean and safe.

These kids pick up trash in a river.

These kids sort trash in their community.

Helping Habitats

People are not the only living things that share our public spaces. Many plants and animals live in forests, parks, and the ocean. You can help these plants and animals by keeping their habitats, or homes, clean.

Everyone can pitch in and help keep public spaces clean. Do not throw trash on the ground. If you do, you are breaking the law. Trash must be placed in a trash can. If you see trash on the ground, throw it away! Try to leave places looking better than they did when you got there.

Recycle

People can help their communities by **recycling**. This means taking used items and turning them into something new. There are many items that can be recycled. Glass, cans, and cardboard can be recycled. Even tires can be recycled! They can be used to make new roads.

People can also help by making less trash. There are many ways to do this. One way is to buy reusable water bottles instead of plastic ones. Another way is to use reusable cloth bags at stores. That keeps lots of plastic bags from being thrown away. Small changes like these can make a big difference!

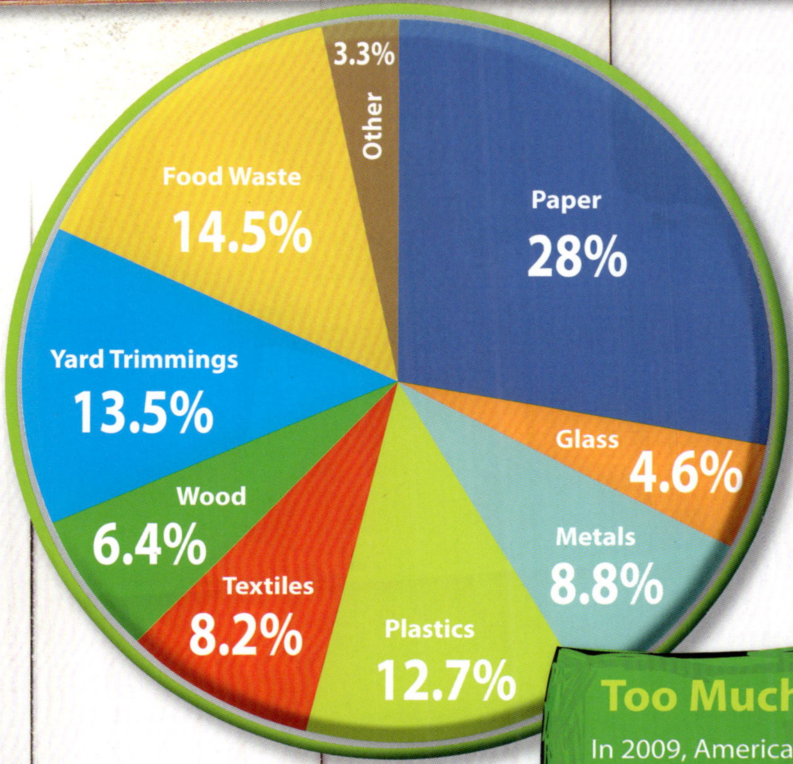

This pie chart shows the percentage of materials in Americans' trash each year.

Too Much Trash!

In 2009, Americans made enough trash to circle Earth 24 times! This is just one reason why it is important to recycle. We do not want to live on a planet that is covered in trash!

Americans generated about 250 million tons of trash in 2011.

There is 14 billion pounds of trash in the ocean.

This man helps an elderly woman get around town.

Care for Others

Sometimes, certain people need our help. Some of these people are **elderly** (EL-der-lee). These are people who are our older citizens. As people get older, some things become harder to do. Some elderly people are not able to see as well as they once did. They may have to stop driving. So they need help going to the store or to the doctor.

Some elderly people live far away from their families. Sometimes, they get lonely. You can help by visiting them. They have many fun stories to tell. Elderly people are great teachers. They have learned many things in their lives. And they can teach us about the past.

This girl helps her grandfather with his tie.

This girl helps her grandmother cook.

Some members of communities are not able to help themselves. Animals need protection and care. Good pet owners take care of their pets' needs. But sometimes, animals are not cared for. Pets can get lost, too. Pets are not like wild animals. They do not know how to survive without our care. If pets are lost, people can help return them to their owners. If pets are hurt, people can get them medical help.

Animal **shelters** feed, clean, and play with lost or hurt animals. Your family can donate time and help at the shelters. Or you can **adopt** a pet that does not have a home.

This girl takes good care of her dog.

This woman adopts a cat from a shelter.

Animal Rights

Pets are part of the community. Animals have rights, too. Our country has laws against being mean to animals.

Vote

In America, we get to choose our leaders. We get to be involved in our government. It is our duty to know how our government works. We should know who our leaders are. And we should understand and follow the laws of our country.

Voting is part of being a responsible citizen. When people vote, they choose the leaders for our country. They also decide on the rules and laws for our country. Before people vote, they learn about our leaders and laws. This way, they can make the best choices for America.

These people vote to make a difference.

One day, you will be able to vote. But you can still learn about our leaders today. You can research laws. You can also talk to people about the problems in your community. You can help make a difference!

Voting Laws

You have to be an American citizen to vote. You also have to be at least 18 years old.

Building a Better World

We are all part of communities. We belong to families. We live in neighborhoods. We go to schools. We play together. We work together. Our communities make up our country.

As Americans, we enjoy many freedoms. We can be happy and safe. We have the right to speak freely. We can believe what we want. But we also have responsibilities. The best way to protect our freedom is by being good citizens. We can do this by helping our communities.

We need to follow the laws. We need to take care of one another. We need to respect one another. We all have to do our part. This keeps our communities strong. If we work together, we can build a better world for everyone.

Try It!

There are many different things you can do to improve your community. You can help a neighbor. You can clean up a park. You can volunteer at an animal shelter. Find something that interests you. Find a way to make a difference. Then get out there and do it!

These kids donate their old clothes.

This family cares for one another.

These boys clean up their community.

Glossary

adopt—to legally take as one's own

charities—organizations that help people in need

citizens—people who legally belong to a country

donate—to give something to help a person or an organization

elderly—older, past middle age

natural disasters—sudden and terrible events in nature

public—able to be used by anyone

recycling—making something new from something that has been used before

relief—things such as money, food, or medicine that are given to help people in need

responsibilities—tasks or duties that are required

rights—things a person should be allowed to have or to do

shelters—places that provide food and protection for people or animals that need help

volunteers—people who work without getting paid

Index

Your Turn!

Be a Role Model

Being a good citizen means helping your community. How are you a good citizen? Make a list of all the ways you help your community. Then, share your list with others. Be a good role model. This will inspire other people to do the same.